I0726963

SEX

WITH MY FAMILY

FICTIONS

JESSICA ANNE

Published by Long Day Press
Chicago, Il 60647
LongDayPress.com
@LongDayPress

ISBN: 9781950987306

Library of Congress Control Number: 2023931974

Layout by Joshua Bohnsack

Printed in the United States of America
First Edition

PROUD MEMBER
[clmp]

What mold do you make of me to pour your elixir, your fluid into, and then reward?

The bunny mold? The kitten mold? The flower mold? The damaged flower mold? Pregnant at twelve, illiterate, but with a twist? The gay mold? The white trash mold? The battered child mold? The bad girl mold?

— Carole Maso

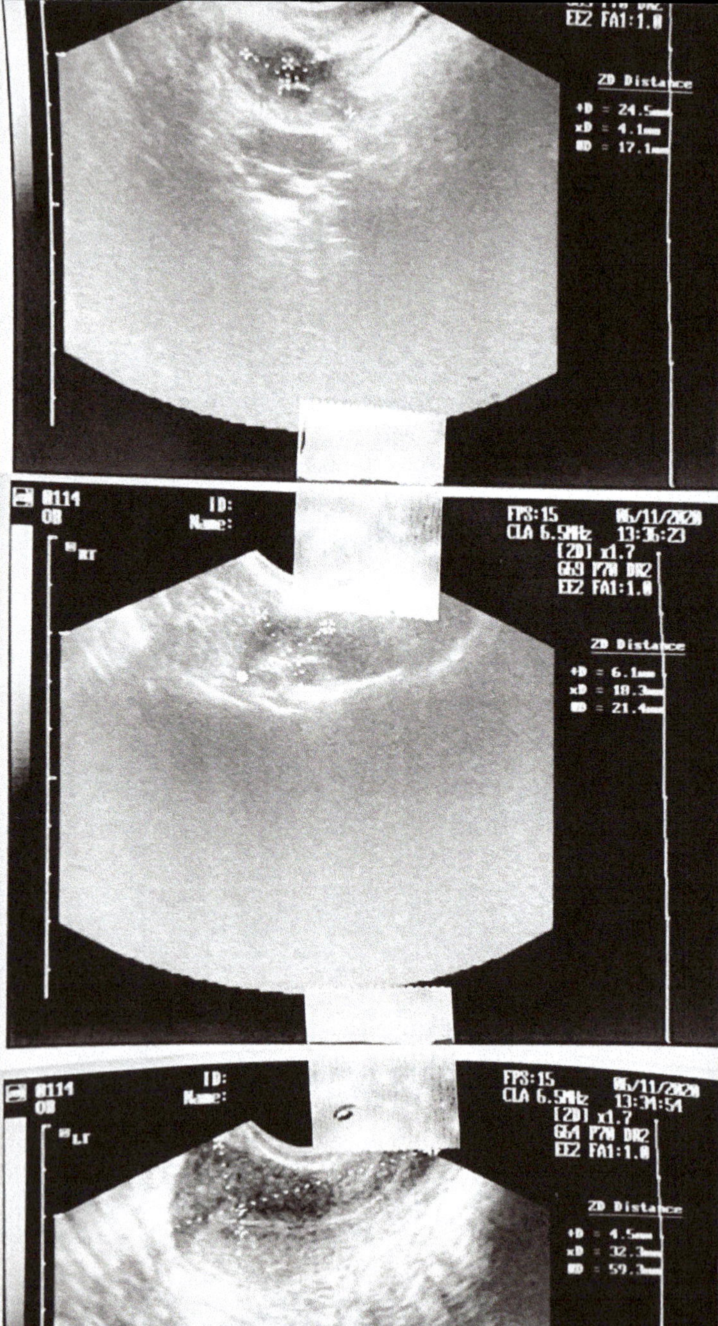
EE2 FA1:1.0
2D Distance
+D = 24.5
xD = 4.1
D = 17.1
0114
OB
ID:
Name:
FPS:15 06/11/2020
CLA 6.5MHz 13:36:23
[2D] x1.7
G69 P70 DR2
EE2 FA1:1.0
RT
2D Distance
+D = 6.1
xD = 18.3
D = 21.4
0114
OB
ID:
Name:
FPS:15 06/11/2020
CLA 6.5MHz 13:34:54
[2D] x1.7
G64 P70 DR2
EE2 FA1:1.0
LT
2D Distance
+D = 4.5
xD = 32.3
D = 59.3

While you were booking a hotel, I was starving. While I was at our appointment, you were in a hotel (a nurse's aide held my hand). You wouldn't tell me where your hotel was or when you were coming home. You didn't want your sperm collected, I guess. You didn't want my eggs, it seemed. You left the empty jar on the stool by the door. You left a note on the dresser. I lost the floor. You said in your note you didn't want the baby. I explained to Megan, there is no baby. That's the whole problem. There's been no baby for years. That's why we're here. I lost the floor and dialed Megan. You wouldn't answer your phone, (in your letter you said to call a friend if I needed help). I called Tim. I couldn't eat for twelve hours, so I called Tim. You called your mom. I texted your mom. Oh, fuck. I had to find a ride. I found a ride. It wasn't hard to find a ride. You need a ride to and from these procedures, you knew that. You were my ride. Or, die. You knew I had to go in, you knew if I didn't go in my ovaries would explode and I could possibly die. I was surprised your mom texted back. *Please know I love you both.*

Oh, Jesus. Fuck. Tim said I'll be fine. Sarah said I'll enjoy the procedure, she said it's a space dream. I texted Sarah about the procedure. What's it like? I've never gotten this far. The lean, brown busy doctor (the one who put a stack of phone numbers in my palm, looked me in the eye, and said *you will get pregnant this year*) put me to sleep and needled her way up my tube by way of my vagina into my ovary. Just the one. Because this time I only grew follicles on one side, the right side. The goal was to retrieve many eggs. As fine as the needle entered my vein it was my understanding I had eggs to retrieve. I know someone who *donated* her eggs, 50 eggs in one aspiration. You were supposed to produce a load of sperm by masturbation. You signed a piece of paper promising you would ejaculate into a jar. You stabbed the long needle in my ass cheek the night before. You helped me out of the bath. I went to work with a pain in my ass. Then you disappeared. You abandoned us, I went in to freeze the eggs anyway. But, there were no eggs to freeze. After all that, not a single egg. There isn't going to be a baby.

You could have waited in the car. It was a Tuesday.

She, the doctor with magical thoughts, looked me in the eye and told me she wouldn't give up yet.

There I was, alone as I have ever been, groggy from the twilight, understanding nothing. Weeping, reaching for my phone.

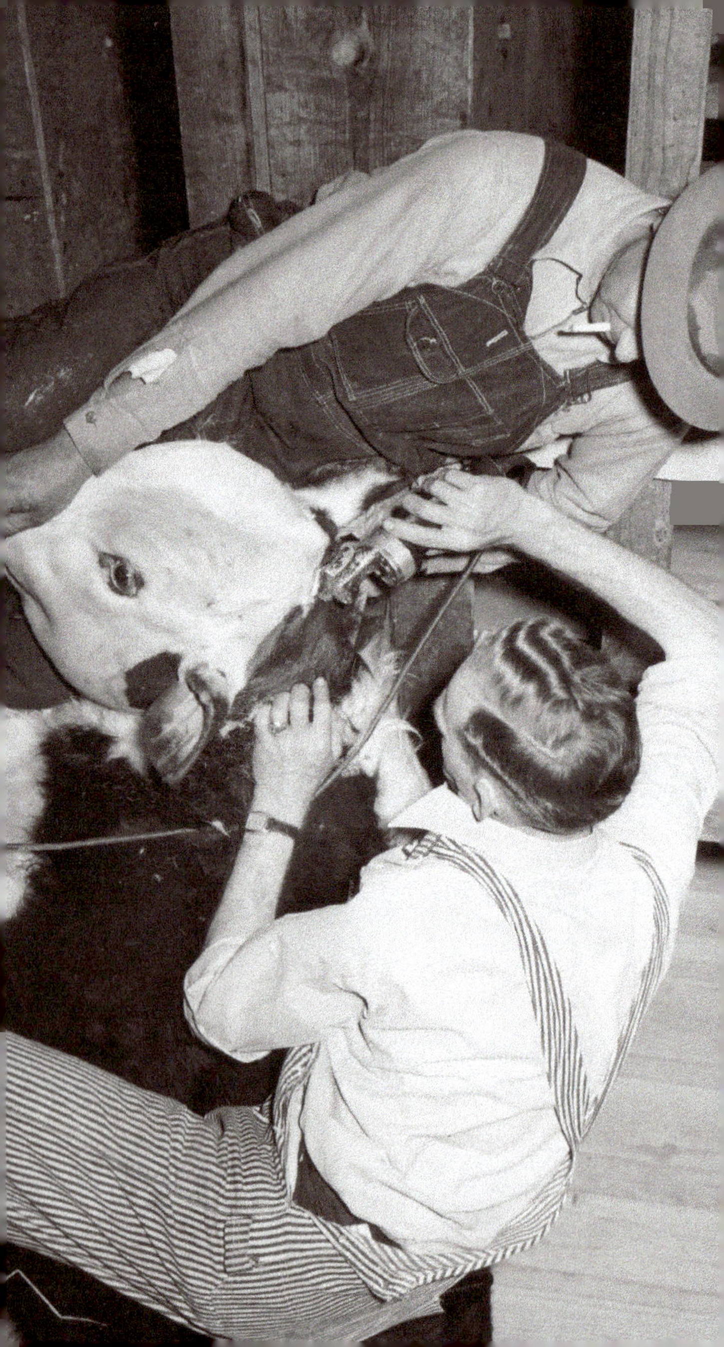

COW

What do you do?

I'm in labor. I'm an artist with jobs, one of them is at a desk. I make things with my body. Various gigs, wigs, and mobile uploads. But I don't wait to be inspired if that's what you're asking. Inspiration is not on the schedule. There is no time to wait around. Every cycle counts. Every hour counts, down.

You can get a lot of writing done during a ten-minute break from labor. You can write your teeth down to the nerves right there in the middle of the day; knees up to your chest, calls crowning, Zooms unfolding. Reports running and accounts clouding.

=====

Because my Family is not as curious as I am about the power of my body, I am alone in this. This, the spin checking portion of my day. Is it clear? Cloudy? Egg white?

I am my own coach and doula. I am seeking my own care, writing my own story, planting my own apple seeds underneath my own tongue.

My Family is not trying to have a baby. But I am trying to have my baby.

=====

Could we start with a list of what I ate yesterday? Or what I remember eating yesterday, rather. I think we just need to get a hold on this. Is anyone taking minutes?

- Rice Krispies Treat that my boss, a single childless woman in her late fifties, made in bulk and brought into the office for us all to share, eat, talk about openly. She is very maternal, the childless boss
- hot Dunkin' coffee with sugar
- can of chicken noodle soup I bought from 7-Eleven on my lunch break and did not heat, ate room temperature directly out of the can. Metal spoon grazing metal rim, little white clouds of fat rising to greet me and my cherry matte lip stain

Then, at the end of the day, when it was dark and I was completely alone in my house, a series of vertical bites.

- bite of plant-based chocolate chip cookie, surprisingly soft
- handful of salt & vinegar chips, Lays
- entire banana
- handful of white shredded cheese
- glass of oat milk to swallow Lexapro

=====

I remember having dinner at a restaurant I could never afford on my own, in my early thirties, with my brothers[1], my step[2] mom[3], and her best friend Gayle, a childless woman in her fifties who never married or dated and was a successful lawyer until the recession when she lost it all but changed careers to psychiatry/counseling/social work, not maternal at all or in the least; this Gayle person. My

1. they were both alive at the time, I think it was their birthday actually[A]
2. their biological
3. divorced from our dad

A. twins

Family was not with me, must have been on stage. But our marriage was new enough that people not only assumed it was okay to talk about if/when/how we were birthing, but also assumed it was okay for me to speak on behalf of Family, as though we were both present.

Without missing a beat, yes. Of course. Three. You know this, you've known me. And you were at the ceremony where we, Family and I, each promised each other and the congregation before us that we would be good parents, better than our own. Never abandon, abuse, neglect.

Without missing a beat, the childless woman called Gayle, staring down at her food, she said *no, no, come on*. She said *Jessica doesn't want kids. She can't have kids.* She forgets she has food on her plate.

Puke-cried in the nice bathroom.

Somewhere in the middle of my labored yesterday of not-for-profit projects and poor diet, I managed to get myself to acupuncture. The acupuncturist told me, reminded me, to eat salmon once a week. And to eat steak once a week.

I am trying to get pregnant with my acupuncturist, myself, and these sacred soft-eyed animals who bring me so much unconditional joy.

Oh, how badly I wish I had a cow! They are so sweet, the cows! Maybe if I had a cow, owned a brown cow, I wouldn't want a baby so bad. Just myself, my family, and my cow on a quiet plot of Michigan land. A barn for the theatre and a quilt for our aging bodies. I could even get a bull for my cow, and breed more cows for the children I don't and might never have. Or my nephews, perhaps my nephews would be happy to inherit my cows. And then my family and I would really feel like we made something together, something sweet and good and for and from the earth.

How magnificent must it be to birth a cow, to see a calf fall from her mother's womb warm and wet.

How could I possibly eat the life I want?

What am I going to do?

There's the Mariano's Market on Lawrence, I could go there, I could walk there, I could ride there and order a cutlet from the man behind the counter. I could ask him to please grill it for me. I could carry it home nestled between my arm and my breast. I could heat it up with a little butter and sea salt. Maybe some mushrooms. I think I have a can. I could eat it slowly and soundly, completely and luxuriously. I have time today. I could finish eating and have the counter scrubbed well before my Family returned from rehearsal. It's a secret, so many secrets; the trying to get pregnant, the meat, the rib separating, heaving desire to birth.

Anyway, I would eat, I would perform all the actions of eating.

And depending on the amount of lines on the stick, I would sex.

I would sex like a heifer. A dewy eyed angry heifer.

Except at this point, the trying, not the sex, but the trying, seems almost as impossible as the conceiving. The dialogue I have with my Family is equal parts grunting, bleating, pawing.

And my eating has spiraled.

I wish I was a cow.

But, how about you? Do you want to have kids? Are you trying?

BUG

Family and I saw a play last night at the local watering hole

I produced the evening,
high hopes.

I saw that Tracy wrote the play, David directed the play, and Carrie was in the play,
names of our household.

Come on, let's pay too much money to sit next to men in tight pants who strike conversations and complain about nothing.

Alone together with our secrets, holding hands!

Two hundred dollars for the tickets, fifty dollars for the drinks & the cheese, eighty dollars on the Ubers

+ I tip high.

Ah! Ummm… (*Sigh.*)

Together in a dark theatre; just watching, not acting. Off the clock. Quietly working some shit out. Trying not to laugh at the nudity, or the land acknowledgement, the harsh light in the fake mini fridge, the kisses without tongues.

Because I worry the thrill is gone.

We used to go wherever the newspaper told us to go.

I worry something has spoiled.

We used to be so happy at the supermarket.

We'd even shop for blankets at the drugstore, pay in cash, drive straight home and take our contacts out of our eyes.

We'd change into our glasses to cut cucumbers into perfect, skinless strips.

Fill our mouths with milk—

The play was bad, but the darkness was just what we needed.

I let myself feel powerful for not having to pay for a babysitter.

I thought about my words and how beautiful our second bedroom is; filled with books, a clean desk, a quiet place to write. No dirty diapers or wet rags. No plastic.

I thought of my baby brother, how sad it was when he stopped showering. Brushing his teeth. Going to class. Calling me back.

I let myself pretend the flicker I felt on my right side was a fertilized egg burrowing deep into my uterus.

I got that sharp pain behind my left breast, I felt a cool flush on my neck and a numbness in my legs, quivering at the back of my throat. It's the oh my god I want my mom feeling that would knock me down if I wasn't already.

Mom? Look at me, just look at me. I don't seem to have any eggs to fertilize; I have slipped on the ultimate middle-aged banana peel. I am sitting in a dark theatre like a 20-year-old, arrested and buzzed. Only eggs I have are scrambled and on my face.

She says yeah, I see. You look pretty. Just try to have fun–even though you're back four hundred dollars watching Carrie Coon smoke electronic cigarettes in the nude opposite a mediocre male actor not listening to a word she says. Just talking to me in your head

in a pretend hotel room.

I think of you whenever I am in a pretend hotel.

And I imagine my baby, here, now, in this dark center aisle. I hold her, trace circles lightly across her back with my thumb. I know she's hungry when she sucks, suckles, suctions her lips hard against my cheek expecting warm milk. I love it when she thinks my face is a boob. I try so hard not to laugh, my one job is to keep the whole family quiet and work some shit out.

They say anything is possible in the theatre, they've been telling me anything is possible in the theatre since before you were even born. Before rideshare, before IVF,

just rocks floating in space.

WHITE KNUCKLED

Knuckles. That's what I remember most from my time, my most recent stint at the fertility clinic up north. Knuckles. The ultrasound technician's knuckles resting against my thigh. That feeling. Like, hi, hands whose mouths I have not kissed. By all means, make yourself at home in there.

Thank God they were not a man. I would have preferred a cow. I would have preferred a water buffalo. I would have preferred my Family. I would have preferred a comfortable chair to be the person inserting the wand, but Jennifer the ultrasound technician, although cold and short with her words, at least presented female.

It was early, before labor.

You have to time it all out with your cycle. Your first morning appointment in a round of IVF needs to be on day three of your cycle. Roughly. I think. No one told me that. But, my instructions were to call when I got my period. And they would ask, *are you at full flow yet?* And then depending on my answer they would schedule an appointment for the next day, or the next next day. Early.

So, when you arrive you immediately have to take off your pants. And your underwear. And your tampon. I made the mistake the first couple of times of just parking my fully-clothed lonely-ass sleep deprived self on the couch, just waiting patiently for someone to come in and take my hand, and acknowledge how broken I felt, ask me where my Family was,

tell. Me. To. Take. Off. My. Pants.

Like, how mortifying is it when Jennifer comes in gobstopped and flustered? *Oh my God, you can get undressed from the waist down and lie down on the table!* Slam. Okay. Thanks for not weighing me I guess.

And, wait. Do I take my tampon out? Where's the trash can? You're just going to stick that lubricated wand camera through my gummed up sausage wallet? I'm bleeding. I'm supposed to be bleeding, right? Can you get blood on your wand? I guess so—

Jennifer just goes for it. No narration. And when

she's tilting the wand left, she rests her right-hand knuckles on the tip top of my naked inner left thigh. I hate it. I want to say please stop. I want to say, can we please take a break, I need to find a more comfortable position.

I wanted my Family, or my calf, or my favorite chair by my side & holding my hand. I wanted to at least be able to look into a loved one's face. Not that Jenny and I were anywhere close to making something, she's just scouting locations here, and I am more screen than person. A pantsless exquisite corpse. Pieces of my bloody uterine lining in the trash can across the room. Naked from the waist down. Winter coat draped across my shoulders. Panties on the couch.

Seems like a lot, like a selfish lot to make a person. My insurance is good and it costs me zero dollars to do IVF, all fertility related diagnosis and treatment is completely covered. And even the medication doesn't set me back any further than my asthma inhalers. It was so easy to be ushered into this world, I never even stopped to seek consent with myself, or my Family. Or did I? What are my choices again?

Of course I would rather adopt, but I have until

I'm 45 to adopt an infant. And I'm only 39. And I would have to borrow money from somewhere, I think. UnitedHealthCarePlusChoice does not cover adoption. And wouldn't I have to speak with that Gayle person if I wanted to adopt? Or someone like that, someone who dismissed me according to my bank account and my BMI. The particulars are not as sheenly presented to me. There's no sans-bougie-serif website for adopting.

But, my heart finds these born, waiting people as I lie here braced against these knuckles. There are plenty of fully formed people, up and walking around. I don't have to do this to my body. If my body can't do this, maybe I should listen to my body. And furthermore listen to all the bodies who also cannot do this right now. But choose to do this right now, this part. It takes a village, tag me in. I wish my insurance covered the transaction of lonely birthed bodies to lonely barren me. I know it's a lot, but I wish Jenny had a bouncing toddler on her hip. I wish I could look into the toddler's eyes and ask her sincerely, would you like to come home with me on the train? I would be able to tell in an instant by the glint in her eye and the curl of her fingers against her palm that she belonged with me. That she was me and I was her. I wish all the options could line up on the same surgical tray. Of course I want to give birth. But, there are lots of ways to give birth. Please, give me birth. Your birth is my birth. My home is open, my blood is spilt.

Why don't you sit up and put your pants on? I'll be right back with some paperwork.

SEED CYCLES

Have you heard of seed cycling?

No, should I be eating seeds?!

Well, you should be paying attention to what
you eat—

...

Are you eating breakfast?

No, no breakfast, not during the week, well, if
my boss brings in cookies, or banana cakes...
I eat the cakes immediately, before 8am. But,
generally, I seem to go a while without eating,
actually. Do you think that affects my levels?
What about fasting? Isn't fasting good for
fertility? I don't take my lunch until 2pm,
so that's like 19 hours I go without eating.
During the labor week anyway.
On the weekends, I let it all hang out—

When did you become such a weekend warrior?

What do you mean?

Well, your schedule. It's so basic these days—

I guess I sold out, wait, seeds?

I don't know, I read a blog.

I told my fertility focused nutritionist I didn't eat breakfast and he looked at me like I just finger banged his cat, so, seeds—

Seeds.

Seeds?

Yeah, some seeds you can eat raw, obviously. Some you have to grind. It's kind of a lot. But if you follow the blog, it tells you exactly what to eat each week, according to your cycle. Your seed cycle.

I want that, blog on top—

And you might want to eat breakfast, pregnant people eat breakfast. And if you want to be pregnant you should act like you're pregnant. They say—

Oh, that I can do. You should see me with my tables—

Pardon?

I've been watching my tables, the rounded edges—

Watching or washing?

Watching.

Watching.

I'm concentrating on my tables.

Okay—

I stare at my tables the way I would stare at a television, or a mirror. I watch them, the rounded edges. The legs. I watch my tables until I feel them. I feel my tables pressing on my pubic bone. Hard. Leaning all their weight.

Dropping. I get wet. I get the urge to push. I turn my head to the side. I close my eyes. I bite down. I am so wide at these tables, the sight of them. So fucking wide. Open. My cervix, my uterus, my canal, my cow; part down the middle. Swim to the bar. Screaming. Make way for my tables, ladies! Step aside, organs! We're playing tables, now! Set it up, Lucy!

Okay—

(Sigh) Like, muffins? Poppy seed?

Um hmm… How many tables do you have?

Three. All my life I wanted a home with three tables.

HE, MY FAMILY

The problem is he signed the paperwork. The thing that trips me up is that all the paperwork is signed and dated. I'd like to point out that we completed the paperwork together, and that we each looped our signatures several hundreds of times on several hundreds of dotted lines. Moreover, the problem here is the paperwork that I have here in my possession, signed. I think it's paramount to consider and should be reflected in the minutes that he, he; my whole Family, and I for that matter, signed and dated the paperwork. The problem, the confusion, comes from the fact that he signed the paperwork.

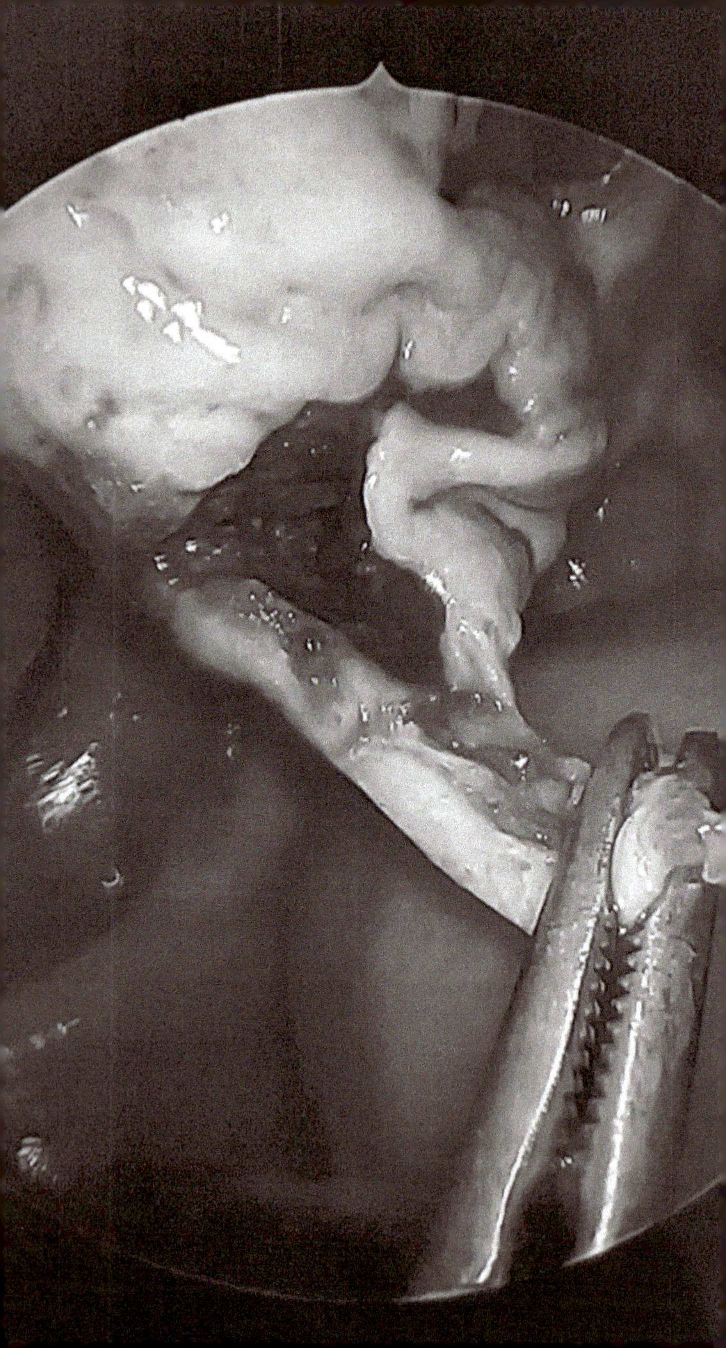

PRODUCE SECTION

1. My traumatic first pap smear, spring 1999. The one where the group of men wheeled in an ultrasound machine, ripped my gown, and joked with each other about how it was not the child of God, haha, look at that, while my first ever speculum was being vaginally inserted by a man who kept saying my name while a woman was drawing a shit load of blood while I cried.
2. All the sex I had with my Family before we had intercourse for the first time. Months of leg sex before I finally spoke up.
3. Ada Grey. I consider the theatre critic, Ada Grey, an integral part of my sexual awakening and reproductive health. And reproductive care.
4. The two couples therapists who refused us care, said, both of them, that we are not ready.
5. My cyst removal.
6. ~~My egg retrieval.~~
7. My trigger shot.
8. My herbs.
9. My gummies.

10. My nephew.
11. The glass containers and the hot baths.
12. The medicine in the fridge, the case in the bathroom, the alcohol swabs on the table. The red container on the toilet. The powder, the solution. The podcasts, the cats, and the texts.
13. The bloating, the headaches, the nausea. The weight, the fights, the cancer, the endo.
14. The top and the bottom.
15. The sticks, the cups, the socks.
16. The heated blankets.
17. The tissues. The caps, the booties, the ties and the straps.
18. The tests, the levels, the voicemails. The speculum inserted up, under, and behind my cervix. The dye injected through the tubes. The balloons at the ends of the tubes.
19. Clomid.
20. Purple beets, red meats, & plenty of sleeps.
21. My sister had an abortion when she was 18 & a baby when she was 19. I hear that, and all I can think is, bitch, you must be so fertile. She also had a baby when she was 30. She said that one was hard, because she was so old. That one was hard, hard on her body. That's my nephew, Nick. My first baby. I held him and rocked him,

fed him and changed him. Every day. He liked Cheerios and books about chicks. His hair was white, but now it's gone.

22. When I'm ovulating, my cervix feels so low I'm afraid I might trip over it.

23. I think of Gilda Radner and Gene Wilder. They say it was Gene who really got her to eat, for the first time. Then she was pregnant. Then she wasn't pregnant. I think of Gilda Radner in that beautiful white flowy gown, on those long, tight legs. Dancing funny circles around that wild and crazy guy. Like a Rockette in February. She did everything right

24. while everyone laughed.

25. It's not fair.

GREEN CARDAMOM

I met an astrology professor at a holiday party. Her name is Allison and her red lipstick does not come off for any reason, she wears white cable knit & studies distant galaxies. Time, light, and the eight minutes it would take our real eyes to realize, adjust to, register that, the sun had switched off, burnt out, exploded into nothing just now and all at once.

She was very pretty and interesting this professor called Allison

I asked her if she believes in God & she left the room. Actually it was a porch. She was cold. A nice man making mulled wine in an antique crock pot in the corner said, I don't see how those two things are related. I said, me either. Really. That's why I ask. Do astrology professors ever specialize in higher powers?

Too late.

But seriously, extinction. There's a reason songs

catch in our heads. We all now belong to a club of unimaginable pain. We have ripped our clothes to shreds and we are seated next to the right hand of the body to contemplate the counterparts of all of existence as we know it gathered here today. There are things we know for certain. Bubbles, and stickers, and kettle corn, for instance. And there is also dust we do not know. And when. When? When? When is a good time for the fiery ball of stars and planets to glitch a stitch of God's hand and blow the entire place up, up, up, and away! Away we sew the buttons on to the snow and carrot our noses under our arms. Is anyone left? Is anyone out there? Beware! Beautiful outlines of bodies swallowed by stars! The astronauts and the argonauts, the apple cakes and the beauty bars cannot will not should not save us from the great big moment within a moment up to the moment of universal reversal. When everything we thought we knew about up, and after, and moment to moment is cut infinite, severed ultimate. She said, you think this is bad? Consider the dinosaurs, consider we're next, consider the dirt beneath your nails left sticky and molded to the galaxy floor. A breath, thousands of years, an octopus. What then? What re-inCARnates then my little shower curtain on a yacht? What tie binds which soul at what table, little miss look at my robes and my books. I'm looking. I like it. I want it. Fill the plain and tall Sarah's of the hour with concerts, and poetry, and lines and circles, leave the energy in good standing for the next organism to evolve into the next creature to rip the next face off. I'm sorry. I know. I promised I wouldn't be mad. I promised you could sleep all night on my chest. I promised I'd see you again. It's just, it's just, it's just, shit gets real real when you enter the great grand mahogany lobby and you drop your red balloon up to the mouth of the bran-ta-soar-me-to-the-kingdom-of-numbers-and-nothings-and why should you want to know? Why are you obsessed with fighting?

So green, so pine, so soft, so empty of time time time that you love-

and it's time time time

the nice man in the muted colors making mulled wine, glogg, if you will, in the corner, surrounded by spices, said, do you cook? I said, I'm not afraid of it. He said, do you want to smell my green cardamom? I said, oh my extinction, yes. Actually, I have to. There is a God! It's not all just random! I'm on a cardamom assignment right now, I need 1,000 words by dawn!

He unhinged a steel, porous ball and placed it softly against my lips like a chalice. I inhaled.

And in that moment I blacked out and smell-sensed only my own shampoo and the smoke from the dwindling bonfire.

But eight minutes later the lavender, licorice, coffee, cinnamon dusted pinecone, mint, leather, CK One, tobacco, musk, cold brew vinegar aroma of his little green sticks hit me first in the right, then in the left nostril

so all powerfully, so transcendent of all understanding that I had to go inside and get some bread and some butter that I do not deserve but am happy to share,

I thought of my dead mother, and the way she smelled when she was covered in snow. I thought of my dead brother and the cheese he liked from Trader Joes.

a high-risk labor and delivery nurse declared 45-year-olds should not give birth! A blonde woman quoted an article in the Atlantic about the rise of antihumanism and someone suggested we sing a Shaker work song, oh, what a gift to be simple, what a gift to be free!

cheers, cheers to the people on the porch and to all a good life!

LATE SUMMER PHOTO DUMP, SOMEWHERE IN CHICAGO

This week in mistakes, (child form text shift command hyperlink subject body) many people died, again, little wooden twigs in their eyes, songs tied to their toes, and podcasts breaking in their waves—

But. Let me ask you this, child form text, who is your dead and have you buried them— yet? Where do they remain? Can I touch it?

This week in mistakes, Meghan McCain posted a pic to her Insta. Did you see it? Did you like it? Did you see the child form text? The blonde bleating pixie swaddled in fatigue. It's supposed to provoke the ones in Alabama Arkansas who agree with her mother and do not remember her father. I keep telling her never to use the first person in child form text. It's bad for her brand. But, she can't hear me over the engine. She says she's depressed, physically ill, broken-hearted and haunted. Oh, no.

This week in mistakes that same little girl with that

same big bellied vacuum sacked hairy white eyeball yellow package of Gluten Free Mussolini Cranberry mix on her sweltering August bound edge of noise and text and guns and pics and tweets she lights a candle and opens her leather-bound copy of *Infinite Jest*. It had to happen. There's a tumor in her vagina and a song in her heart. Give her a break, she's working some stuff out.

It's a good stocked pantry country Saturday buffet to live another day, or at least lace up those creamy discharge green knee socks and sprint up the fly over winding Ravenswood roads like an emotionally unavailable water tower, fisting the air with your prepubescent freckle-stained oh so rounded soft serving shoulder sacks of stone-cold bone, sourly dissecting your relationship to God and literature and foreign relations. You little Hamlet of the north.

This week in missed takes; hormones, needles, full moons and rejections. Wallpaper reams of rejections. Side carrot, ampersand, colon, colon, child form text. Insert. Subject, body, signature, throw a dart. Africa. Alaska. Nether neither Lands, ever heard of 'em? You beef smashing star fucking cameo slinging digital slave hoarder. How's that C list working out for ya, mamma? Kristen Bell have a happy birthday wish for your white ass copper-toned 5th grader? Nice! That's really nice!

"I must be cruel only to be kind; Thus bad begins, and worse remains behind."

—Hamlet

Two can play nice, but three is a biblical bomb squad of whores and markets and lynchings. So where were we? Code up assholes, it's pull out time. Let's see, who can we blame? Was it the underscore, or the asterisks? The backsplash, the squiggle, the guy named Nick Greg Don, the child form text or the stone-cold fossil rocked evil that like it or don't is hooked inside every corner of every cheek.

Whose problem is this? Do we have to keep going? Or should we just call it? Nobody wins the human race. Julia Roberts soils her shoes and horses wear bridles and flowers and ribbons and they get their pictures taken to the newspapers, let's just stop there. There isn't a ballad too high, a Marfa too cracked in the dust, a hashtag stupid enough to balm the crippling anxiety of the children. The children will have to be dragons. Hard to believe through the squeaks of the sneakers in this week's mistakes embedded deep within the child form text a seven-word sentence. The children will have to be dragons. Slipping into the first person for just one more post I am 40 in three months and I have no child form text, but every night I play that same game I've been playing since camp. I push my stomach into my spine and imagine my sister crowning a person and I say a little prayer for the apple cheeks as they crack the crust and unplug the mucus, break through little dragon. Slay, slay the flames and vape the trees. Break the ground and lead the play. Don't be yourself and never forgive. I'm here catching fruit flies and chewing my tongue, find me on Twitter. Rate me to God. Cult me in bars, and string my mistakes.

"I must, like a whore, unpack my heart with words."

—Hamlet

Happy air and water show everybody, talk about a beacon on a hill. A shining city upon a hill whose beacon light guides freedom-loving people everywhere—

"The rest, is silence."

—Hamlet

JESSICA DREAMS POTATOES & CARROTS

How fun, a wedding! Who is wedding, I wonder? Who is wedding today?!

Jessica is wearing a long peach-and-cream toned gown, well, it's more of a slip than a gown. Looks like a nightie, really. Wired bra and crotchless panties shining, glaring through the single silk layer. Like the black pitless eyes of a seat cushion. Should we say something? She looks like she's on her way to get an abortion, or a bikini wax. Maybe she's on her way to work.

She might be *in* the wedding. Black platform shoes? Blue eyeshadow... This outfit is from college. An ill-fitting vintage slip she stole from the costume department. But, why would she steal a slip? Maybe she purchased the slip from the one boutique novelty shop in the middle of town. The one place in the whole town to buy candles and gifts. Bought it with the hourly dollars she made posing nude for figure classes. Always thought there was something odd about buying clothes with that money. Always thought it was weird they paid her in cash at that job.

Someone somewhere must have made a collaged loop of Survivor exit interviews by now.

Good job guys, you got me.

The wedding was in a barn and a church. She was sitting with the musicians. The musicians had instruments to play, but they also had poems to read. Long poems typed up, printed out, and folded in squares. Some time was spent shuffling the papers and then it was her turn to read. But, who is wedding?! When it was her turn to read she read paragraph after paragraph of dense text about the soul in a soft voice while a hundred guests slept either from boredom or the smoke billowing in through the holes in the walls. When she realized she lost the room, she took out a carrot and sliced it into discs. Written in water on each orange slice was a single line of text. She read three rounds then stopped to take a breath and look into the eyes. She could tell the poem was over as quickly as it began and she could tell they liked it and forgave her for the long paragraphs about the soul. She carried the rounds back to her stool and waited for the ceremony to start. The carrots tasted like potatoes, and the percussionist was disappointed. Disappointed about something that wasn't going his way. The wedding never happened and the canary let herself free. Chipped away at the light until the beams couldn't hold.

My Family cannot ejaculate into the cup. He can ejaculate into me. But not the cup.

The disappointments are eating her alive, nothing can be controlled anymore. If you run out of champagne at your wedding, you send your brother to the store. If the rent goes up, you pay it.

=====

It's like acne. It hurts. Deep, stubborn mounds of dirt. Revved up bright as a fire truck. It won't kill you, but it will kill you.

=====

I woke up barely remembering the hazed edges of the three lines of poetry printed on my three pieces of dream carrot. Grasping. Casting. Bloody knuckles. It might be a message, hold. Hold.

=====

And then it was too late. All I remember now is *friend*. The word 'friend' was repeated three times.

ACKNOWLEDGMENTS

Thank you Hart Lang for the assignment and space in which these pieces first appeared in performance. Thank you Long Day Press for publishing something so slim and strange. Thanks Christian for the blurb. Thank you my Nebraska Writing Group for plague-workshopping. This book, all books, are for my brother, Alex, in memoriam.

Jessica Anne is Neo-Futurist, Lit & Luz artistic associate, author of *A Manual for Nothing*, and Visiting Lecturer at Roosevelt University.

A NOTE ON THE TEXT

The ornamental text used is **IBM Plex Mono**, an international typeface family designed by Mike Abbink, Paul van der Laan, and Pieter van Rosmalen, IBM BX&D, in collaboration with Bold Monday, an independent Dutch type foundry. Plex was designed to capture IBM's spirit and history, and to illustrate the unique relationship between mankind and machine.

The body text is set in **Adobe Calson Pro**. William Caslon released his first typefaces in 1722. Caslon's types were based on seventeenth-century Dutch old-style designs, which were then used extensively in England. For her Caslon revival, designer Carol Twombly studied specimen pages printed by William Caslon between 1734 and 1770.

IMAGES

P.1 Lee, Russell. "Cattle, Cruzen Ranch, Valley County, Idaho." *The New York Public Library Digital Collections*. 1941.

P.8 Jessica Anne's ovaries, resting.

P.12 Lee, Russell. "Cowboys clipping a Hereford steer which will be shown in the San Angelo Fat Stock Show. San Angelo, Texas." *The New York Public Library Digital Collections*. 1940.

P.28 Lee, Russell. "Herd of cattle at feeding trough near Crystal City, Texas." *The New York Public Library Digital Collections*. 1939.

P.32 Lee, Russell. "Bull's head. Cruzen Ranch, Valley County, Idaho." *The New York Public Library Digital Collections*. 1941.

P.34 Jessica Anne's left ovary during cyst removal, surgery.

P.38 Lee, Russell. "Cattle and attendants in the stockyards at Aledo, Illinois." *The New York Public Library Digital Collections*. 1937.

P.44 Lee, Russell. "Hereford cattle eating hay grown by flood irrigation methods in the Little Colorado River Valley in Apache County near Springerville, Arizona." *The New York Public Library Digital Collections*. 1940.

P.57 Jessica Anne as toddler, probably 1985. Probably shot by CW: mother's drug dealer; also photographer, childless, kept birds.

Long Day Press

New & Forthcoming Titles

An Atavic Fear of Hailstorms
João Reis

I Will Teach You Retribution
Timothy Moore

Girl Thing
Morghen Tidd

Discord, a Regression
Christian TeBordo

Memory Field
Eric Tyler Benick

www.ingramcontent.com/pod-product-compliance
Lightning Source LLC
Chambersburg PA
CBHW040235170726
48295CB00014B/928

* 9 7 8 1 9 5 0 9 8 7 3 0 6 *